BASS RECORDED VERSIONS

incubus Morni...

"Mexico" has been omitted due to the absence of bass.

Music transcriptions by Steve Gorenberg

ISBN 0-634-06492-4

HAL•LEONARD® CORPORATION

7777 W. BLUEMOUND RD. P.O. BOX 13819 MILWAUKEE, WI 53213

In Australia Contact:
Hal Leonard Australia Pty. Ltd.
22 Taunton Drive P.O. Box 5130
Cheltenham East, 3192 Victoria, Australia
Email: ausadmin@halleonard.com

Visit Hal Leonard Online at
www.halleonard.com

Nice to Know You

Words and Music by Brandon Boyd, Michael Einziger, Alex Katunich, Jose Pasillas II and Chris Kilmore

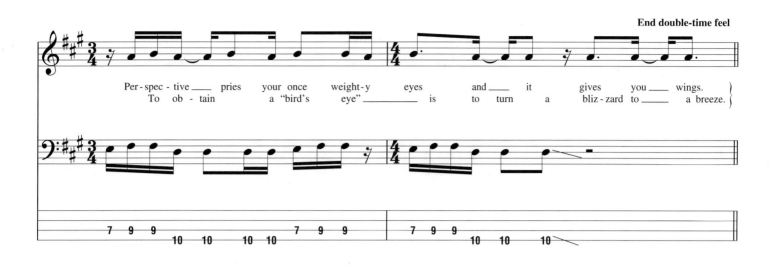

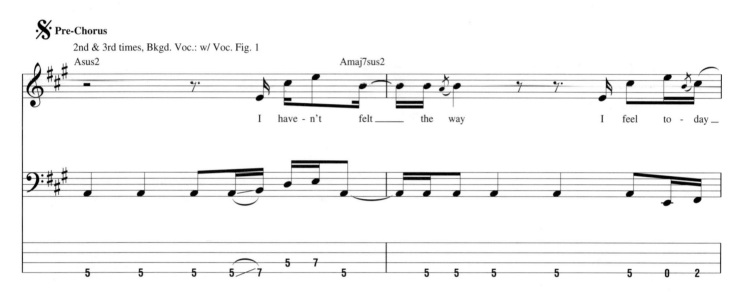

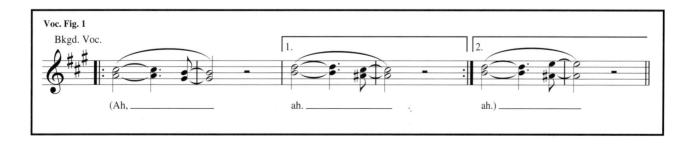

Chorus

Double-time feel

1st time, Bass: w/ Bass Fig. 2 (4 times)
2nd & 3rd times, Bass: w/ Bass Fig. 2 (3 times)

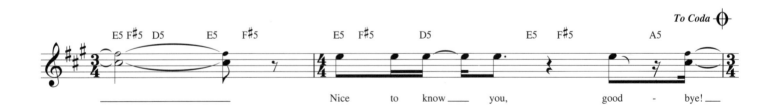

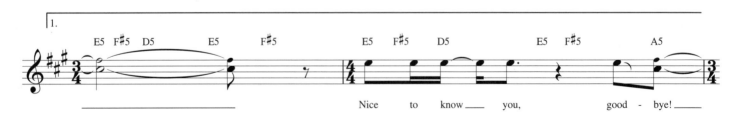

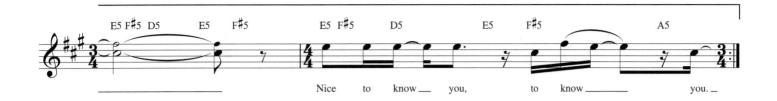

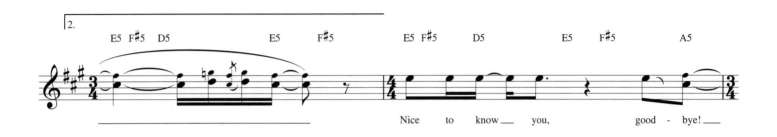

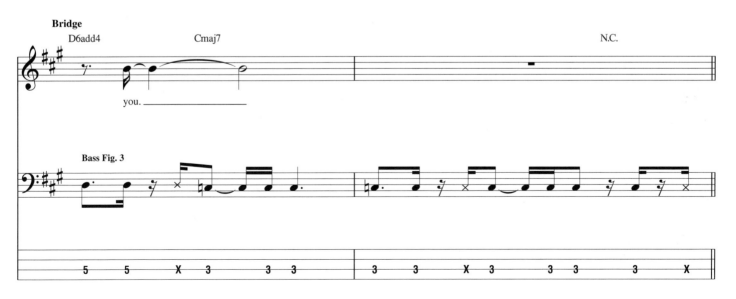

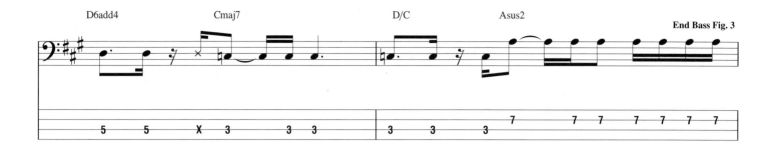

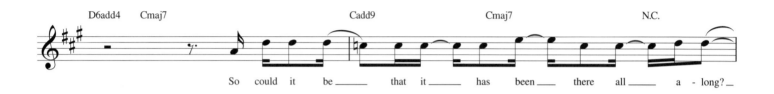

So could it be _____ that it _____ has been _____ there all _____ a - long? _____

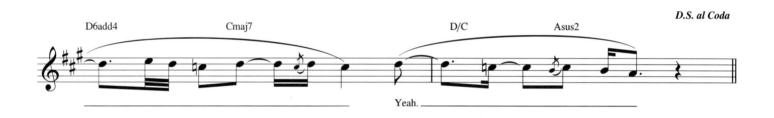

Yeah. _____

⊕ Coda

Nice to know _____ you, good - bye! _____

Nice to know _____ you, to know _____ you. _____

Circles

Words and Music by Brandon Boyd, Michael Einziger, Alex Katunich, Jose Pasillas II and Chris Kilmore

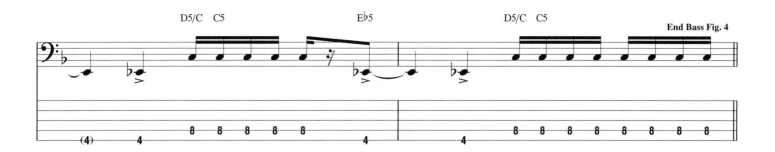

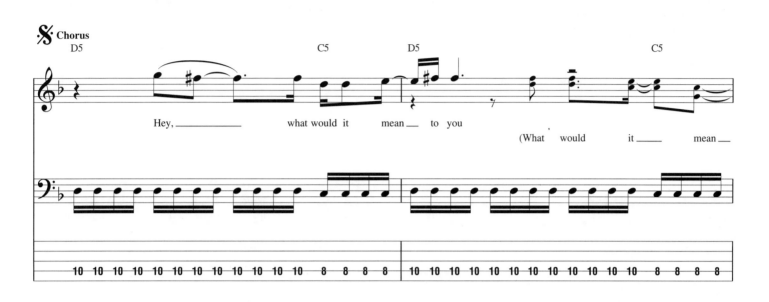

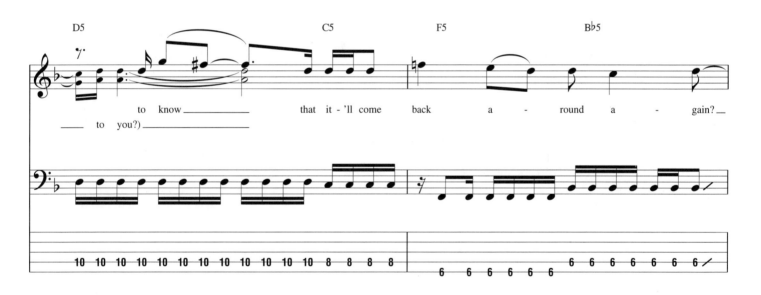

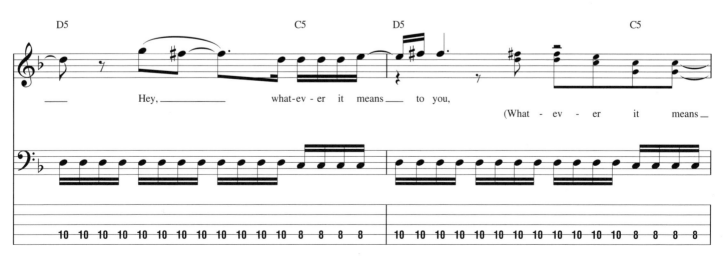

9

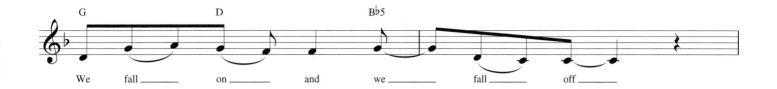

We fall ____ on ____ and we ____ fall ____ off ____

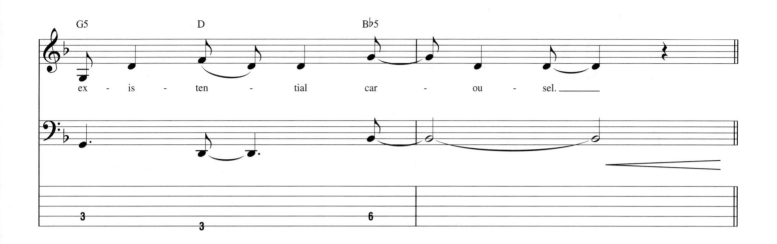

ex - is - ten - tial car - ou - sel. ____

D.S. al Coda

Bass: w/ Bass Fig. 4

Spin!

Coda

Outro

Bass: w/ Bass Fill 1

Bass: w/ Bass Fig. 1

moves in ____ cir - cles, yeah. ____

Oh, ev - 'ry - thing moves in cir - cles. Round ____

Bass: w/ Bass Fig. 2 (2 times)

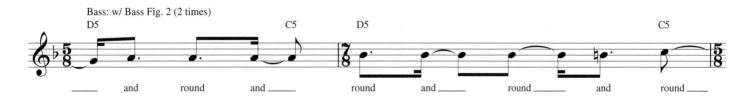

____ and round and ____ round and ____ round ____ and round ____

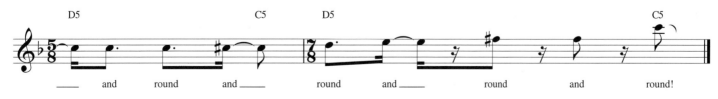

____ and round and ____ round and ____ round and round!

Wish You Were Here

Words and Music by Brandon Boyd, Michael Einziger, Alex Katunich, Jose Pasillas II and Chris Kilmore

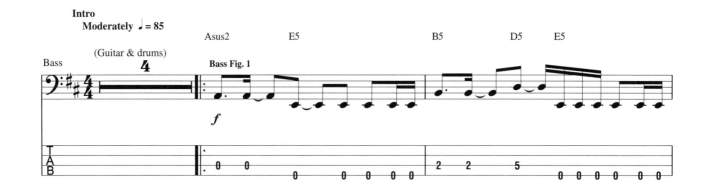

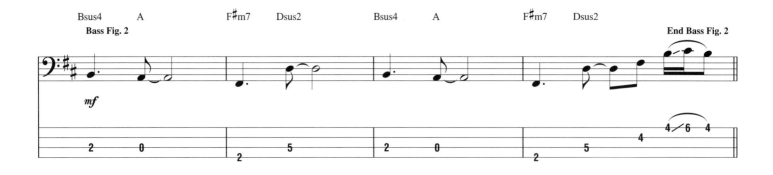

1. I dig___ my toes___ in - to___ the sand.___

The o - cean looks___ like a thou - sand dia - monds___ strewn a - cross___ a blue blan - ket.

I lean __ a - gainst __ the wind, __ pre - tend - in' I __ am weight - less.

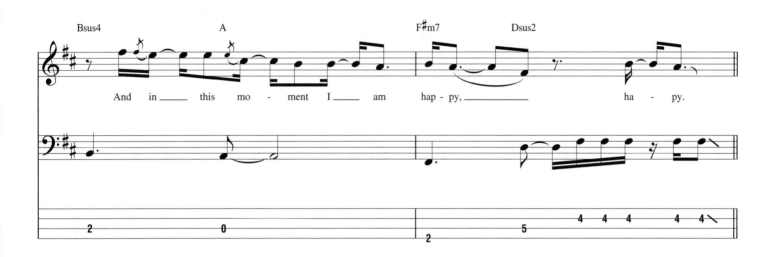

And in __ this mo - ment I __ am hap - py, __ ha - py.

Chorus
Bass: w/ Bass Fig. 1

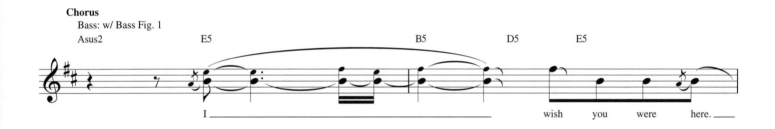

I __ wish you were here. __

__ I __ wish __ you were here. __

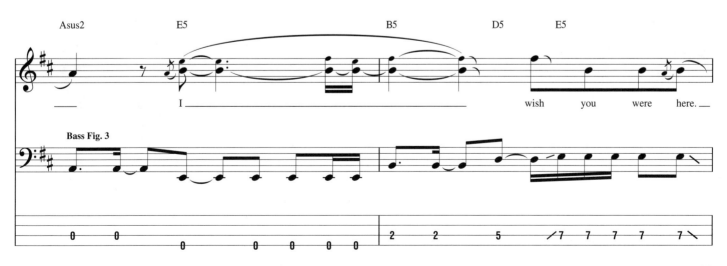

__ I __ wish you were here. __

Bass Fig. 3

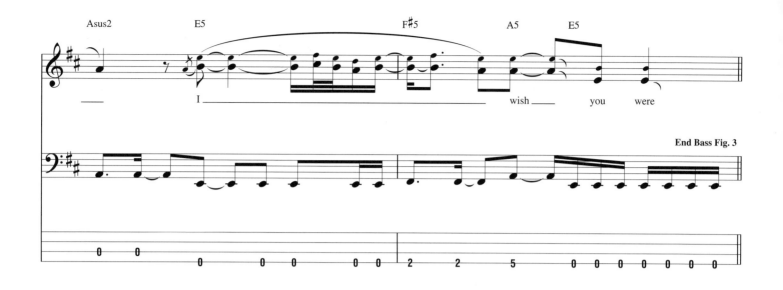

I _____ wish ___ you were

End Bass Fig. 3

Interlude

Bass: w/ Bass Fig. 2

here. ___

Verse

2. I lay ___ my head ___ on - to ___ the sand. ___

The sky re - sem - bles a back - lit can - o - py ___ with holes ___ punched in it.

I'm count-ing U. F. O.'s, I sig-nal them with my light-er,

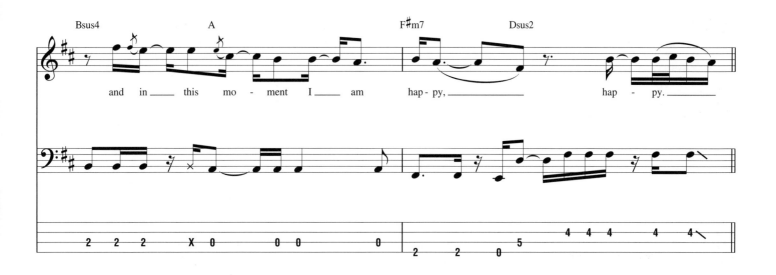

and in this mo-ment I am hap-py, hap-py.

Chorus

Bass: w/ Bass Fig. 1

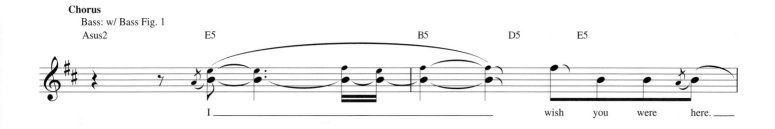

I wish you were here.

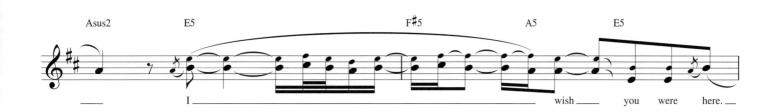

I wish you were here.

Bass: w/ Bass Fig. 3

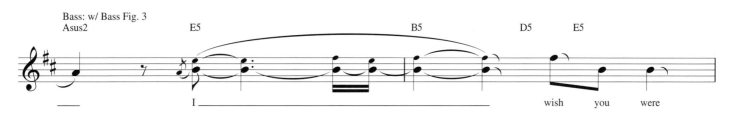

I wish you were

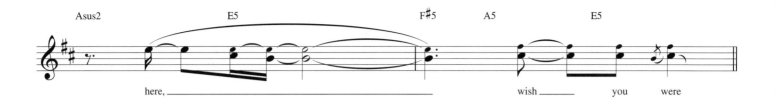

here,_____ wish_____ you were

Interlude

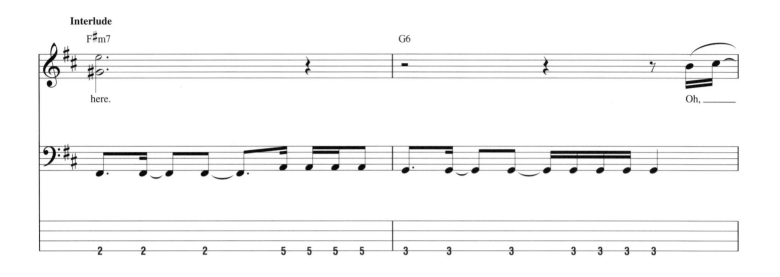

here.

Oh,_____

_____ yeah,_____ oh._____

Bridge

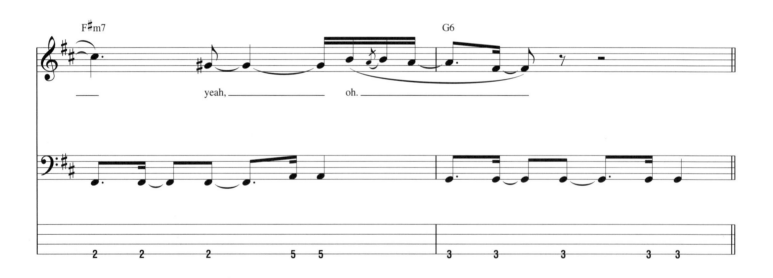
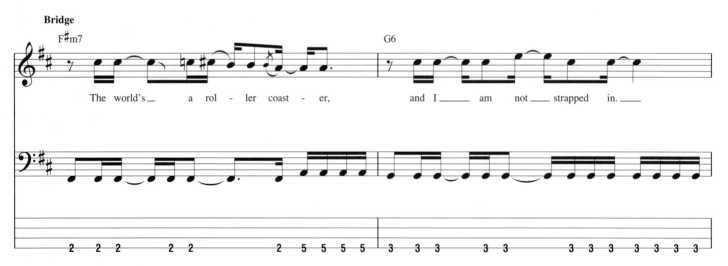

The world's__ a rol - ler coast - er, and I____ am not___ strapped in.____

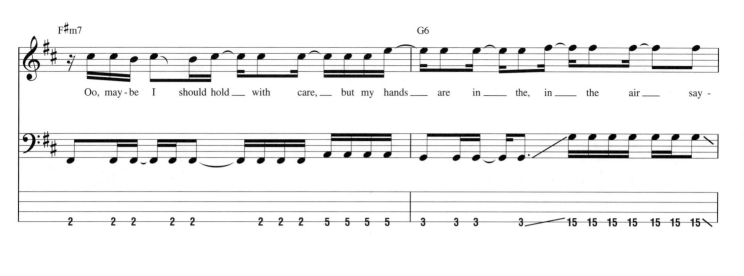

Chorus

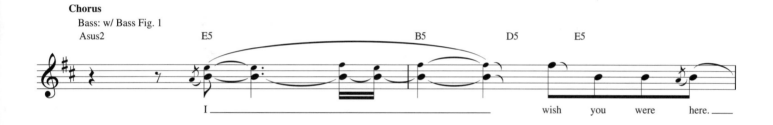

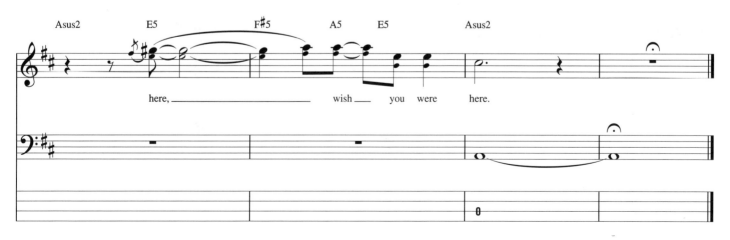

Just a Phase

Words and Music by Brandon Boyd, Michael Einziger, Alex Katunich, Jose Pasillas II and Chris Kilmore

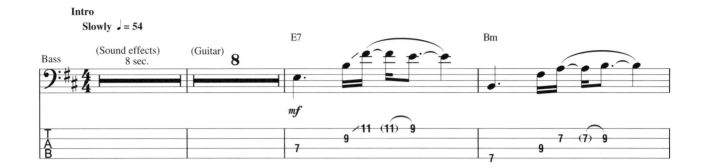

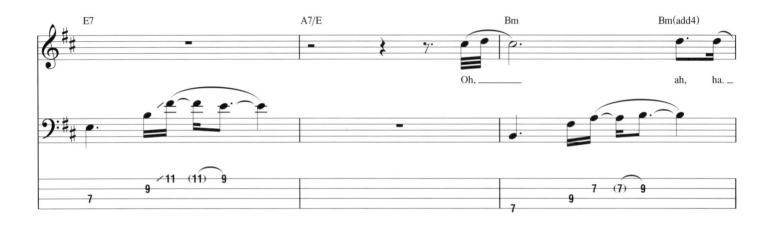

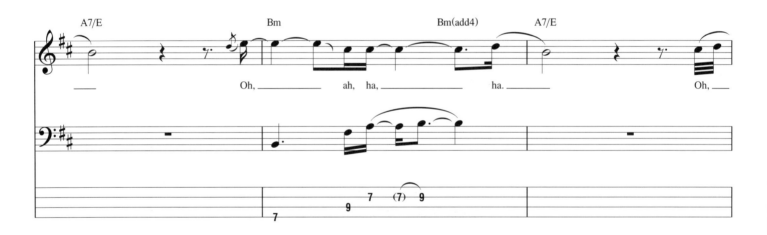

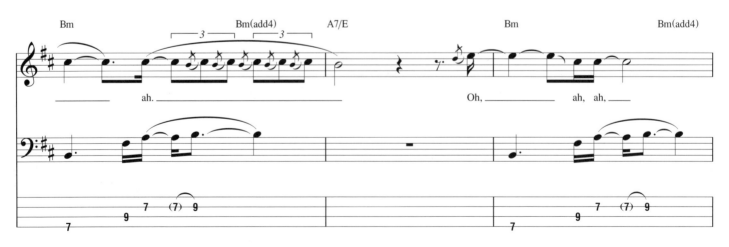

*Percussive slap with fingers.

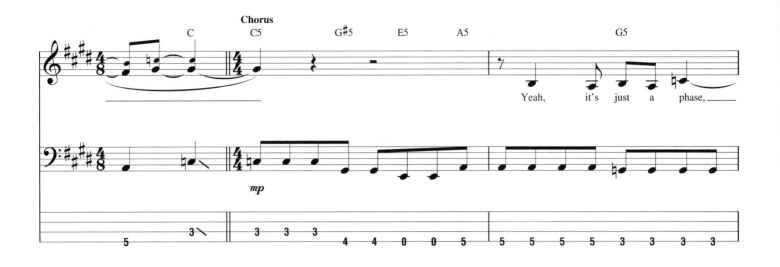

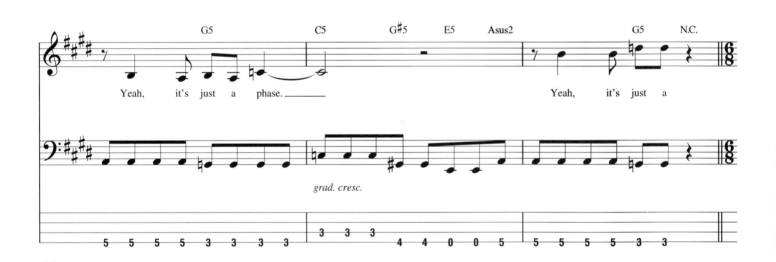

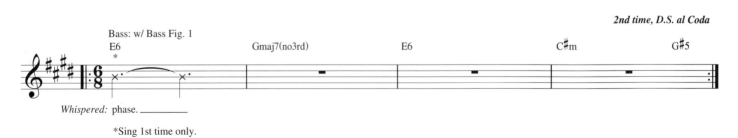

22

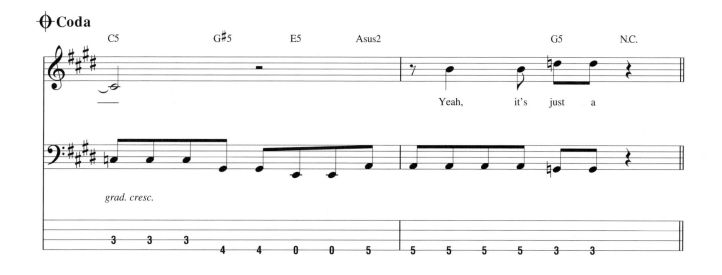

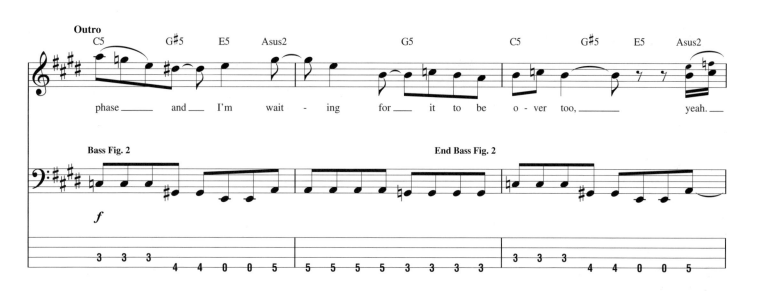

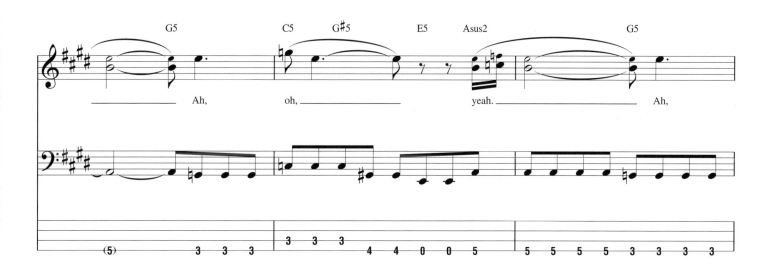

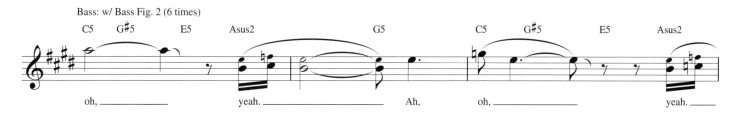

Ah, oh, _____ yeah. _____ Ah,
(Ooh, _____ ooh.

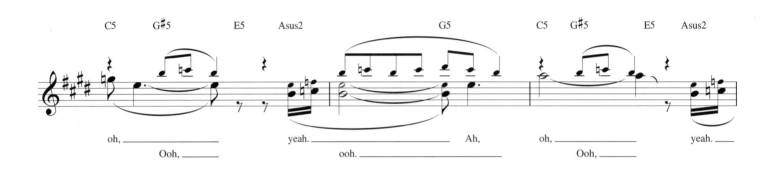

oh, _____ yeah. _____ Ah, oh, _____ yeah. _____
Ooh, _____ ooh. _____ Ooh, _____

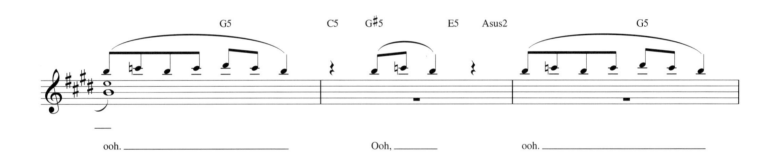

ooh. _____ Ooh, _____ ooh. _____

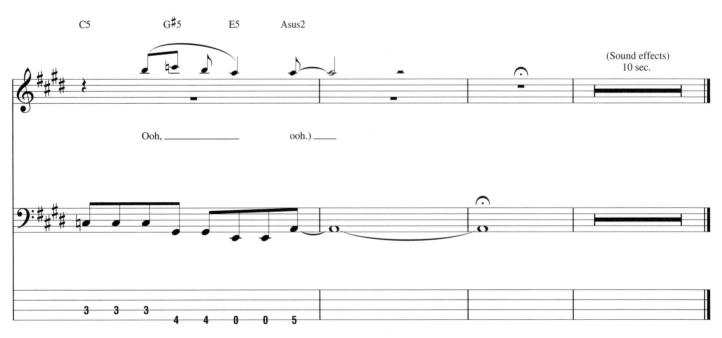

Ooh, _____ ooh.) _____

11am

Words and Music by Brandon Boyd, Michael Einziger, Alex Katunich, Jose Pasillas II and Chris Kilmore

cred-its tra-verse_ sig-ni-fy-ing the end_ but I missed_ the best part. Could we_ please go back to the

Pre-Chorus

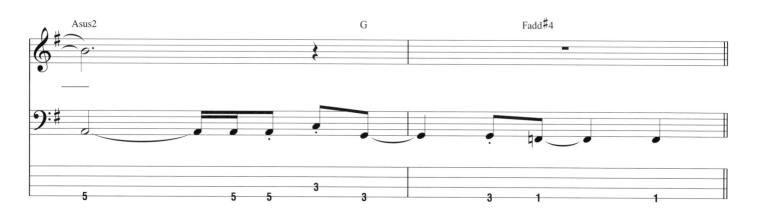

start? For - give my in - de - ci - sion._

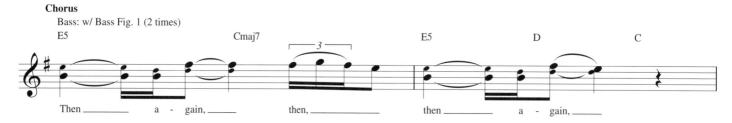

Chorus
Bass: w/ Bass Fig. 1 (2 times)

Then ____ a - gain, ____ then, ____ then ____ a - gain, ____

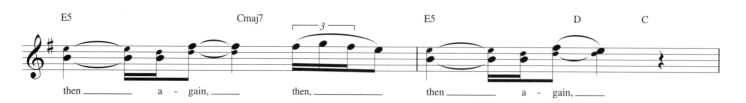

then ____ a - gain, ____ you're al - ways first. __ when no __ one's on __ your side. __ But

then ____ a - gain, ____ then, ____ then ____ a - gain, ____

then ____ a - gain, ____ a day will come __ when I __ want off __ that ride, __ yeah. __

Verse
Bass: w/ Bass Fig. 2

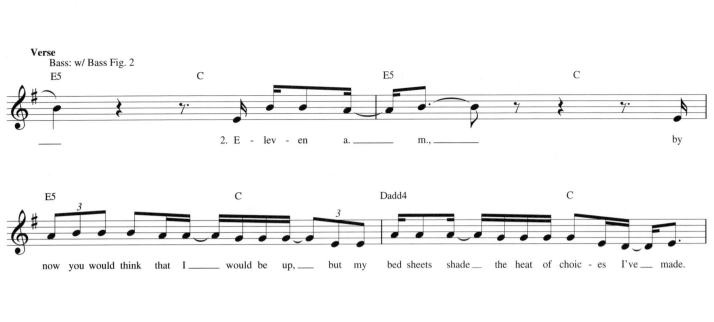

2. E - lev - en a. m., by

now you would think that I would be up, but my bed sheets shade the heat of choic - es I've made.

And, what did I find? I

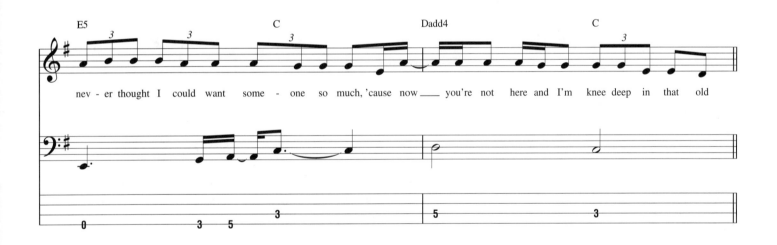

nev - er thought I could want some - one so much, 'cause now you're not here and I'm knee deep in that old

Pre-Chorus

fear. For - give my in - de - ci - sion.

I am on - ly a man.

Chorus
Bass: w/ Bass Fig. 1 (2 times)

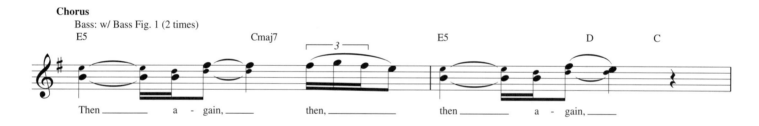

Then a - gain, then, then a - gain,

then a - gain, you're al - ways first when no one's on your side. But

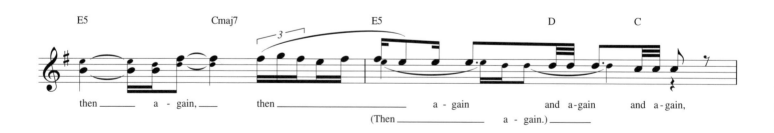

then a - gain, then a - gain and a-gain and a-gain,
(Then a - gain.)

then a - gain, the day will come when I want off that ride, ba -

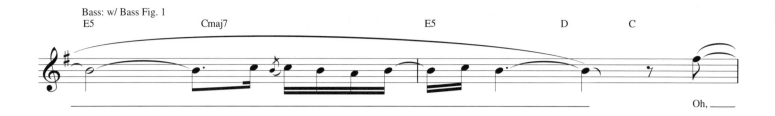

Bass: w/ Bass Fig. 1

Oh, ____

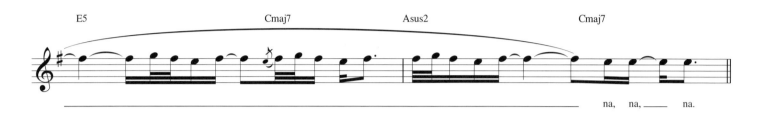

na, na, ____ na.

Outro-Chorus

Bass: w/ Bass Fig. 1 (2 times)

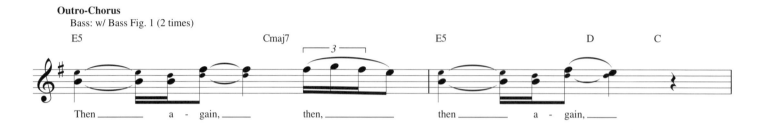

Then ____ a - gain, ____ then, ____ then ____ a - gain, ____

then ____ a - gain, ____ you're al - ways first ____ when no ____ one's on ____ your side. ____ But

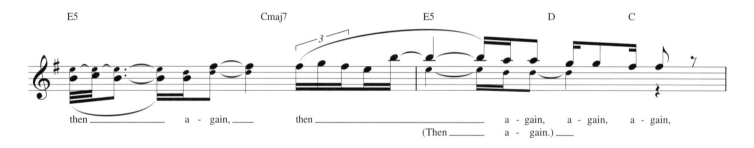

then ____ a - gain, ____ then ____ a - gain, a - gain, a - gain,
(Then ____ a - gain.) ____

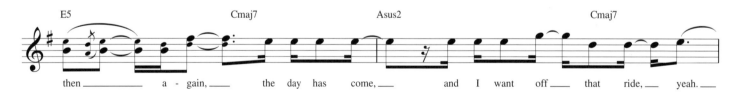

then ____ a - gain, ____ the day has come, ____ and I want off ____ that ride, ____ yeah. ____

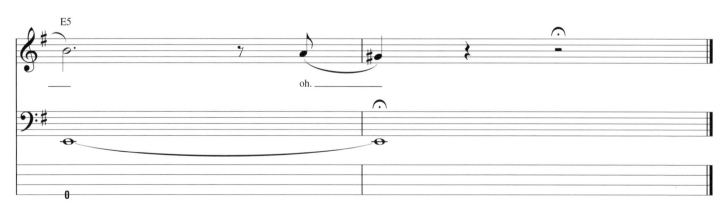

____ oh. ____

Blood on the Ground

Words and Music by Brandon Boyd, Michael Einziger, Alex Katunich, Jose Pasillas II and Chris Kilmore

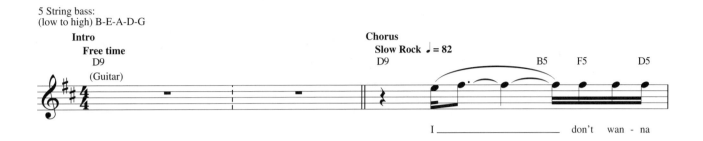

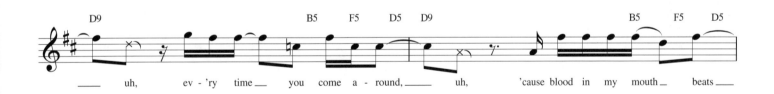

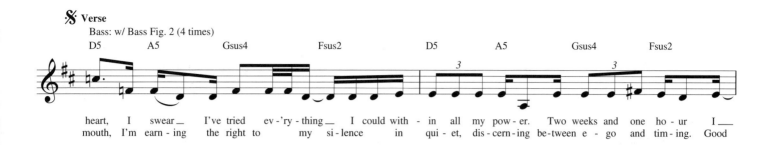

Verse

Bass: w/ Bass Fig. 2 (4 times)

D5   A5   Gsus4   Fsus2   D5   A5   Gsus4   Fsus2

heart, I swear__ I've tried ev-'ry-thing__ I could with - in all my pow - er. Two weeks and one ho - ur I__
mouth, I'm earn - ing the right to my si - lence in qui - et, dis - cern-ing be-tween e - go and tim - ing. Good

D5   A5   Gsus4   Fsus2   D5   A5   Gsus4   Fsus2

__ slaved and now I've got noth-ing to show. Oh, if on - ly you'd grow tall - er than a __ brick wall.__ From now
judg-ment is once a - gain prov-ing to me __ that it's still _____ worth its weight__ in gold. __ From now

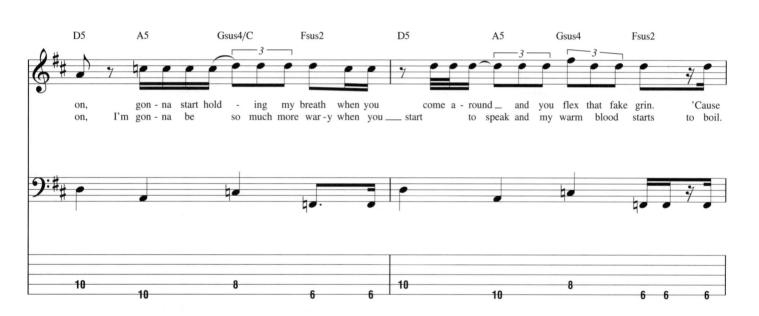

D5   A5   Gsus4/C   Fsus2   D5   A5   Gsus4   Fsus2

on, gon - na start hold - ing my breath when you come a - round__ and you flex that fake grin. 'Cause
on, I'm gon - na be so much more war-y when you __ start to speak and my warm blood starts to boil.

To Coda 1

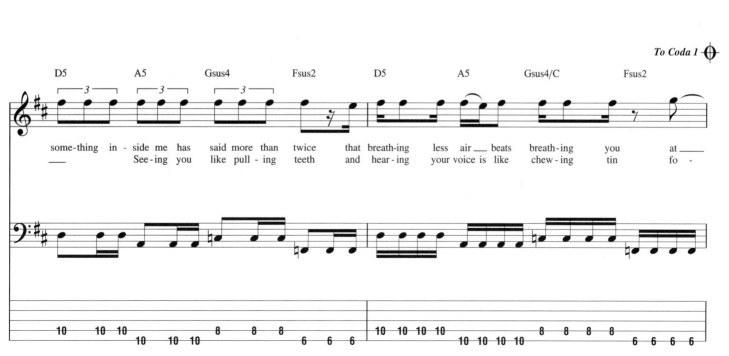

D5   A5   Gsus4   Fsus2   D5   A5   Gsus4/C   Fsus2

some-thing in - side me has said more than twice that breath-ing less air __ beats breath-ing you at _____
__ See-ing you like pull - ing teeth and hear-ing your voice is like chew-ing tin fo -

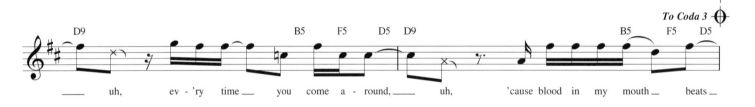

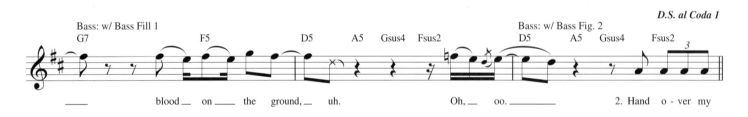

Coda 1

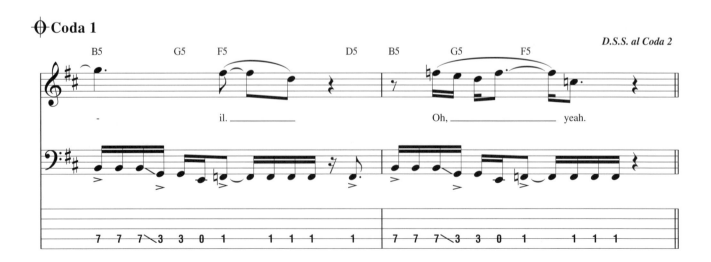

A, by say-ing less __ to-day, _____ I will __ gain more, _____

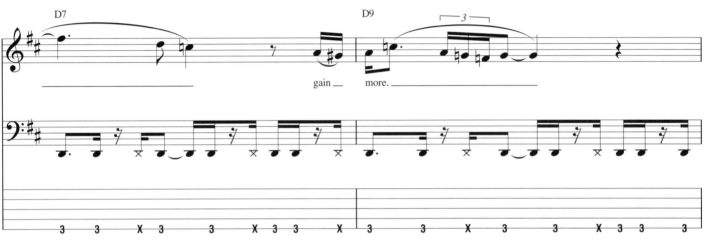

gain __ more. _____

Low twos to you __ my, _____ my __ fick - le friend, __

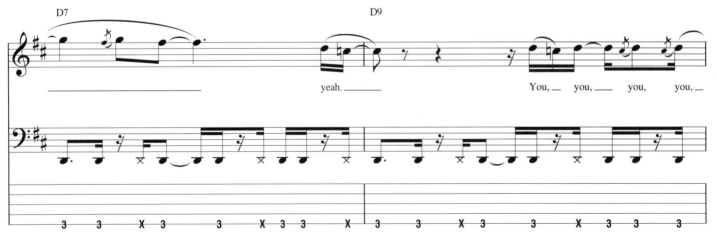

yeah. _____ You, __ you, __ you, __ you, __

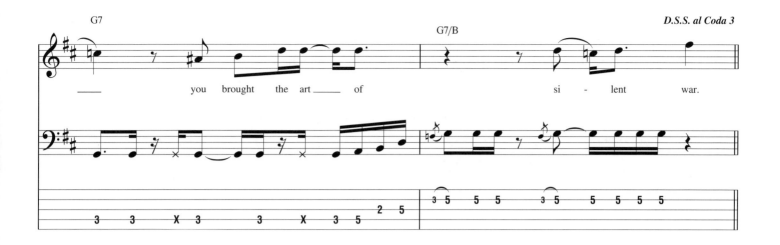

you brought the art ___ of si - lent war.

⊕ Coda 3

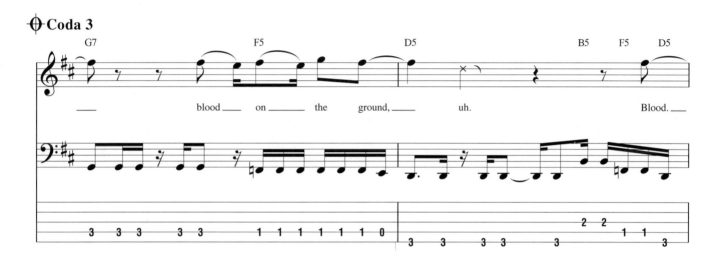

___ blood ___ on ___ the ground, ___ uh. Blood. ___

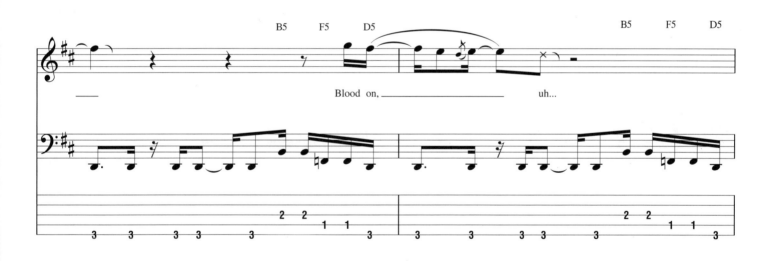

___ Blood on, ___ uh...

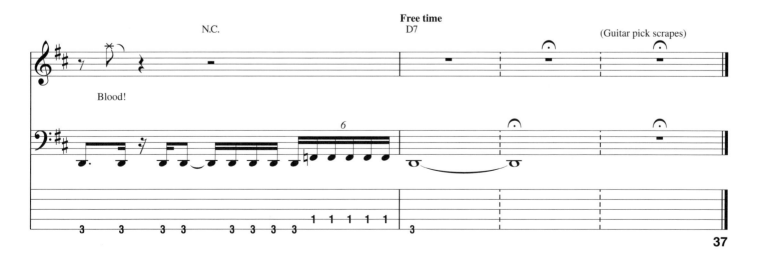

Blood!

Warning

Words and Music by Brandon Boyd, Michael Einziger, Alex Katunich, Jose Pasillas II and Chris Kilmore

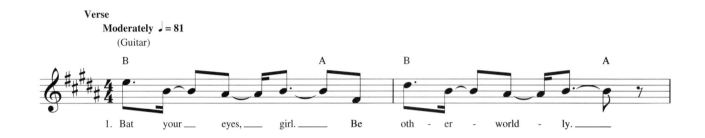

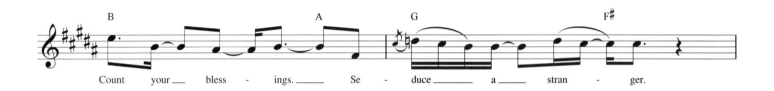

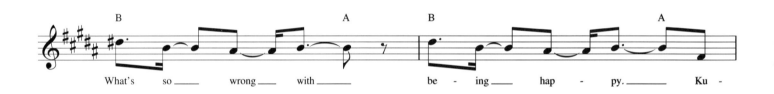

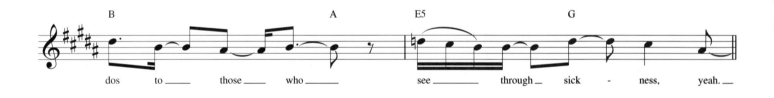

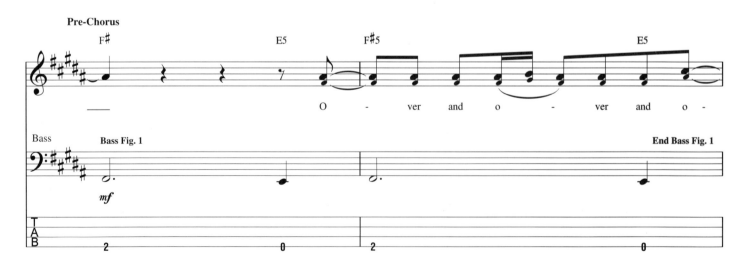

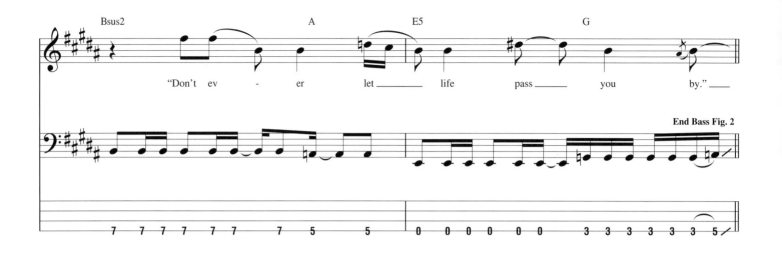

"Don't ev - er let life pass you by."

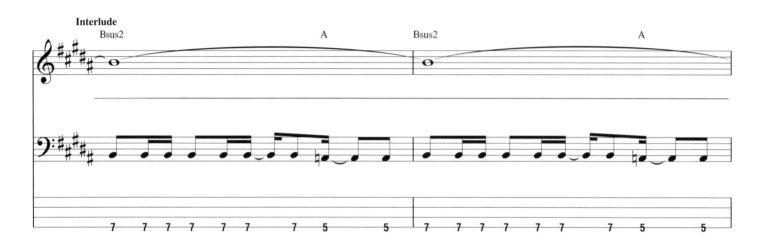

Interlude

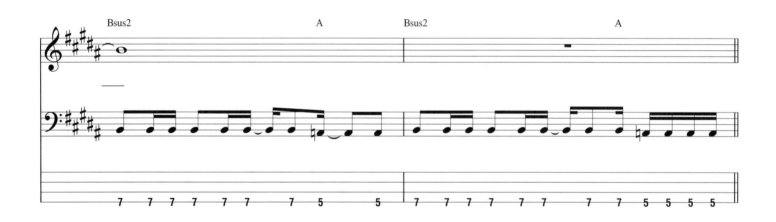

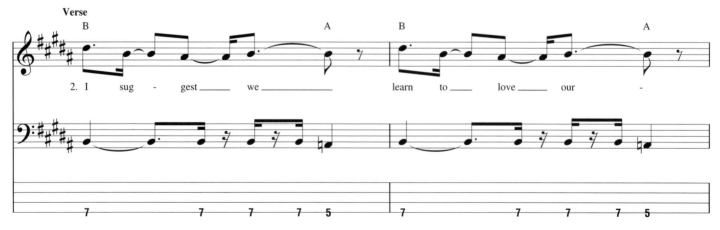

Verse

2. I sug - gest we learn to love our -

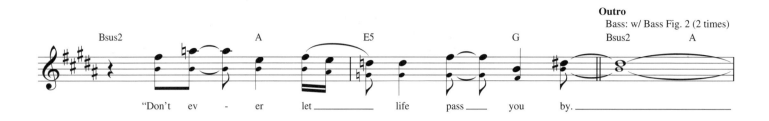

"Don't ev - er let _____ life pass _____ you by. _____

_____ pass _____ you by." _____

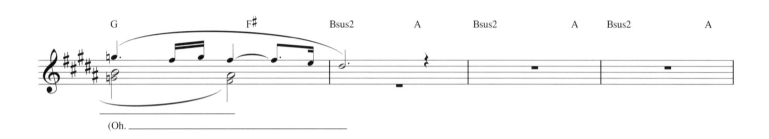

(Oh. _____

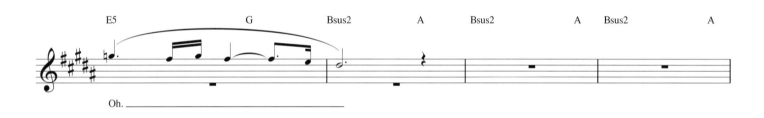

Oh. _____

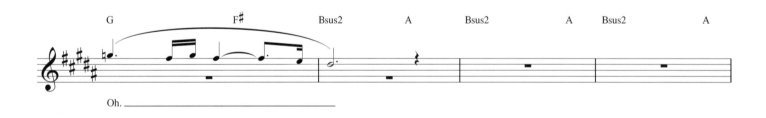

Oh. _____

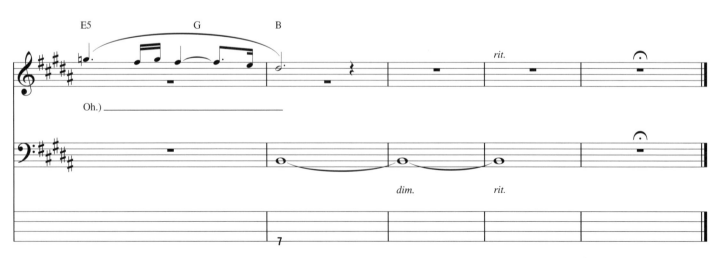

Oh.) _____

44

Echo

Words and Music by Brandon Boyd, Michael Einziger, Alex Katunich, Jose Pasillas II and Chris Kilmore

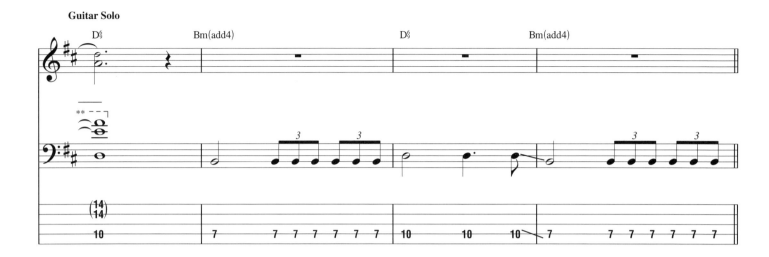

Guitar Solo

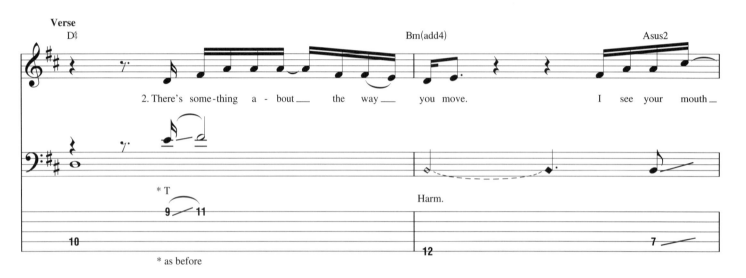

Verse

2. There's some-thing a - bout ___ the way ___ you move. ___ I see your mouth ___

* as before

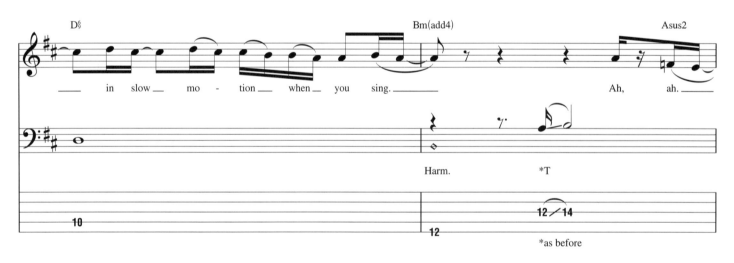

___ in slow ___ mo - tion ___ when ___ you sing. ___ Ah, ___ ah. ___

*as before

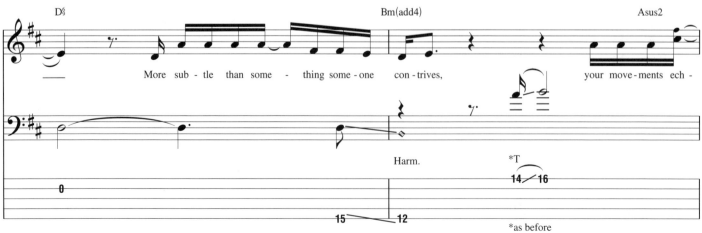

More sub - tle than some - thing some - one con - trives, ___ your move - ments ech -

*as before

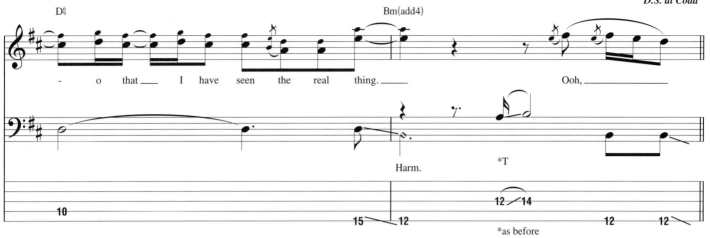

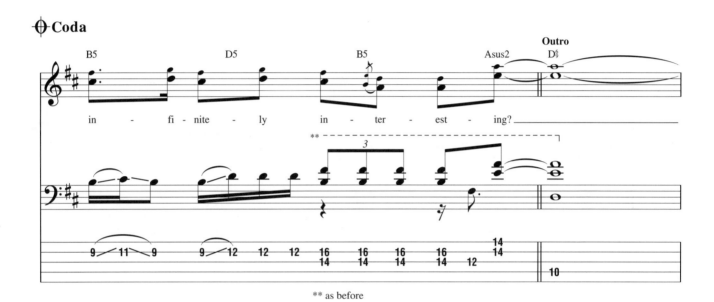

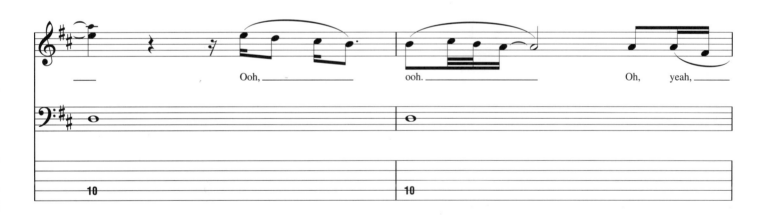

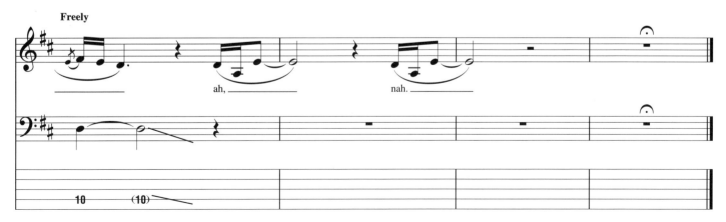

Have You Ever

Words and Music by Brandon Boyd, Michael Einziger, Alex Katunich, Jose Pasillas II and Chris Kilmore

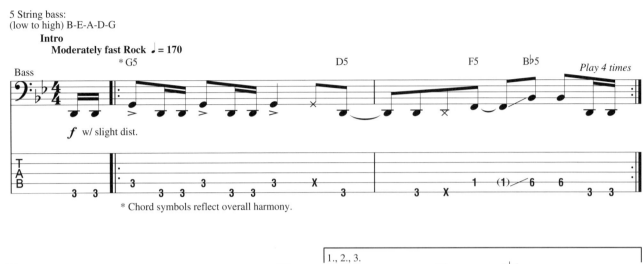

* Chord symbols reflect overall harmony.

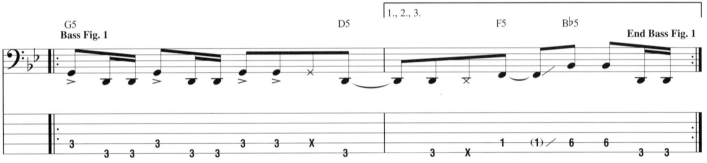

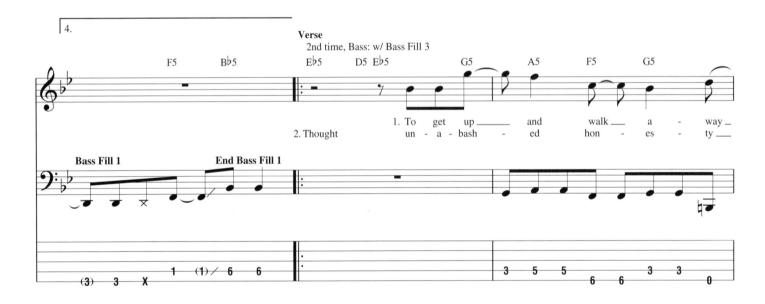

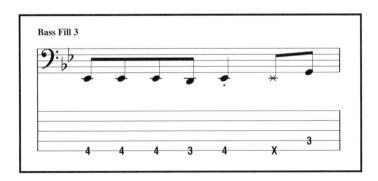

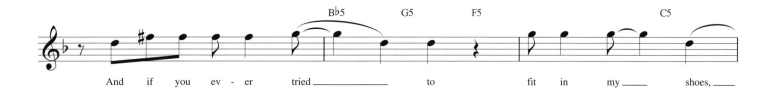

And if you ev - er tried ___ to fit in my ___ shoes, ___

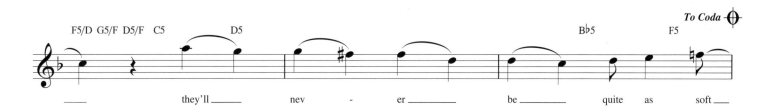

___ they'll ___ nev - er ___ be ___ quite as soft ___

To Coda

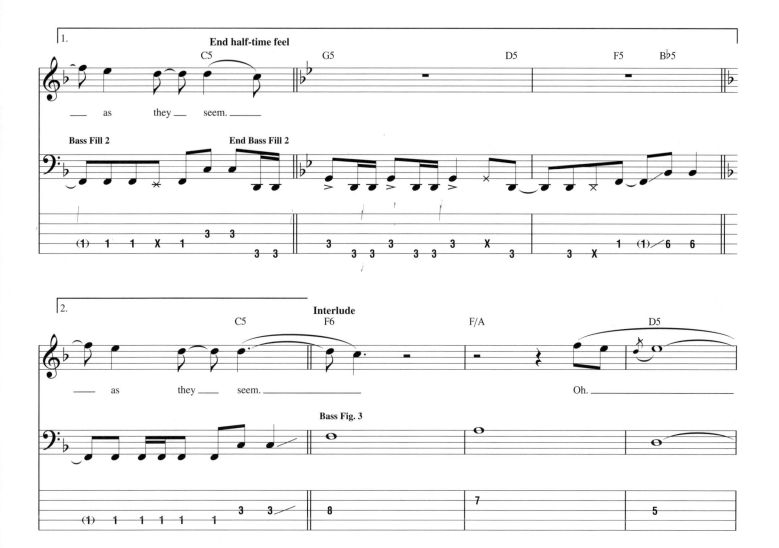

1.

End half-time feel

___ as they ___ seem. ___

Bass Fill 2 **End Bass Fill 2**

2.

Interlude

___ as they ___ seem. ___ Oh. ___

Bass Fig. 3

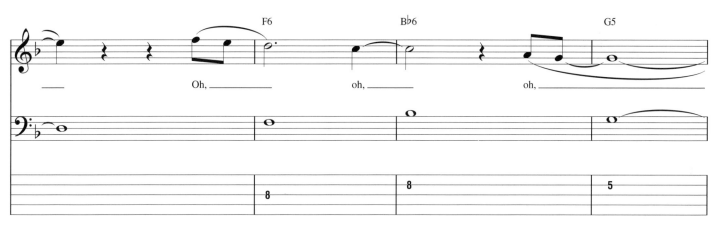

___ Oh, ___ oh, ___ oh, ___

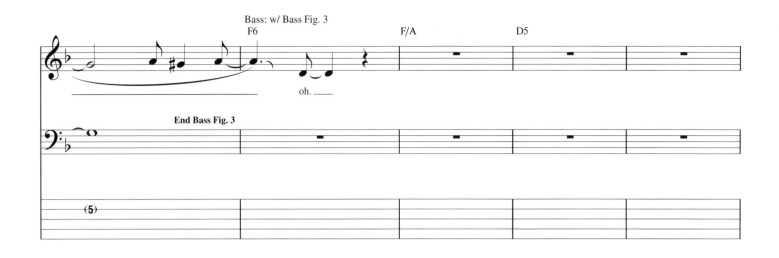

Oo. _____

Bridge

Have you ev - er, have you ev - er tried ___

___ to? ___ I have nev - er,

D.S. al Coda

I have nev - er tried _____ to!

⊕ Coda

Outro
End half-time feel

___ as they ___ seem. _____

Oo!

Are You In?

Words and Music by Brandon Boyd, Michael Einziger, Alex Katunich, Jose Pasillas II and Chris Kilmore

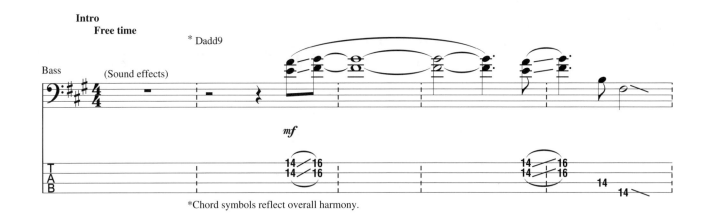

*Chord symbols reflect overall harmony.

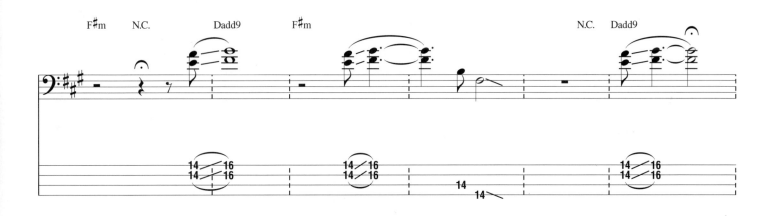

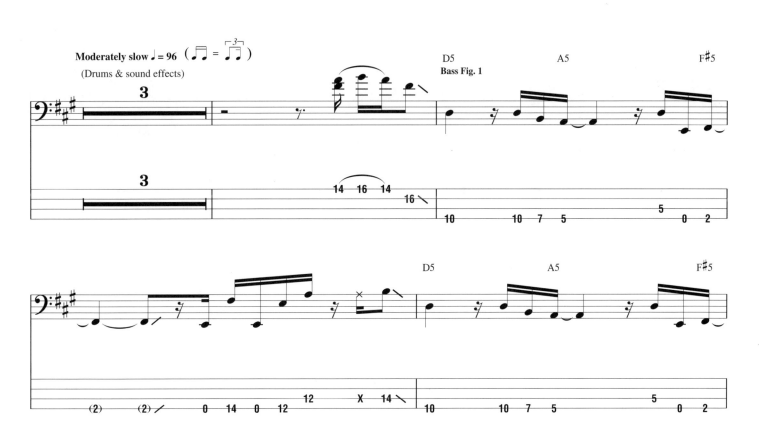

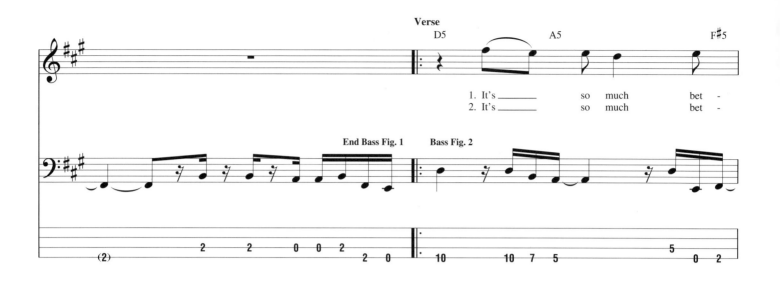

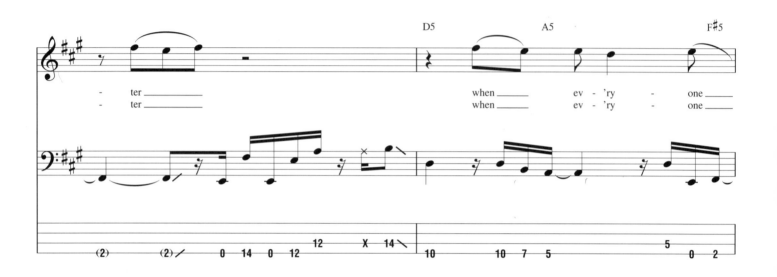

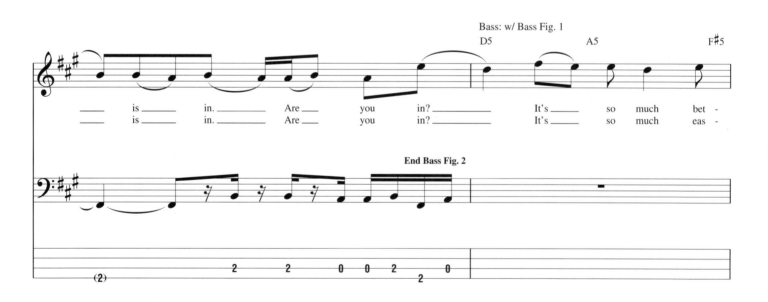

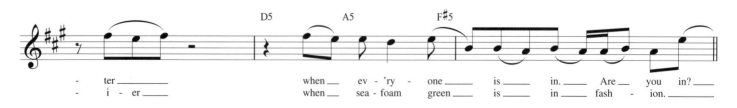

Under My Umbrella

Words and Music by Brandon Boyd, Michael Einziger, Alex Katunich, Jose Pasillas II and Chris Kilmore

I can see _____ for miles. _____
I re - mem - ber why _____ I smile. _____

There's com - fort in _____ my dark _____ seat, _____
Un - der my um - brel - la, _____

and cha - os in _____ the aisles. _____
I'm an ac - comp - lished ex - ile. _____

Chorus

1st & 2nd times, Bass: w/ Bass Fig. 1 (1 1/2 times)
3rd time, Bass: w/ Bass Fill 1

3rd time, Bass: w/ Bass Fig. 1 (last 6 meas.)

N.C.(F)   Db

These eyes are not _____ your eyes, _____ and these eyes are not _____ the col -

F   Ab   Db5 Eb5 Db5

- or that _____ your ar - id eyes _____ might be. _____

3rd time, Bass: w/ Bass Fig. 1 (1st 4 meas.)

N.C.(F)   Db

No, I was not _____ a - round, _____ when those eyes of yours _____ de - cid -

Bass Fill 1

61

Aqueous Transmission

Words and Music by Brandon Boyd, Michael Einziger, Alex Katunich, Jose Pasillas II and Chris Kilmore

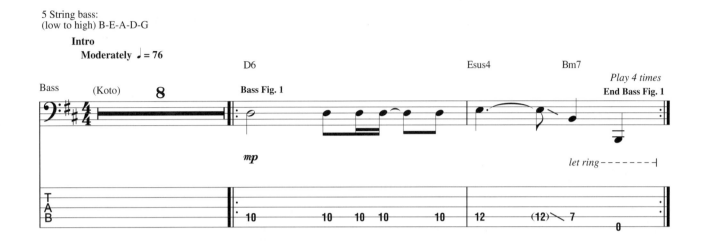

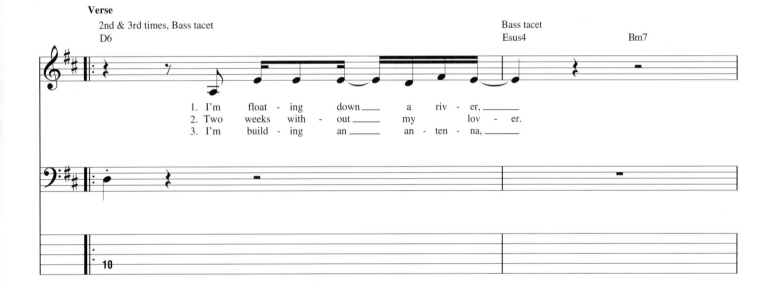

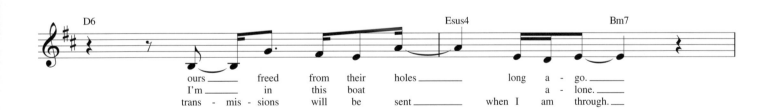

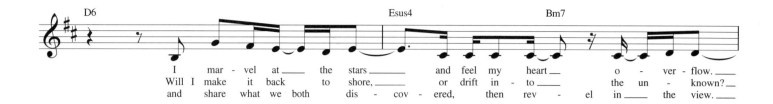

I marvel at the stars and feel my heart overflow.
Will I make it back to shore, or drift into the unknown?
and share what we both discovered, then revel in the view.

Chorus
Bass: w/ Bass Fig. 1 (4 times)

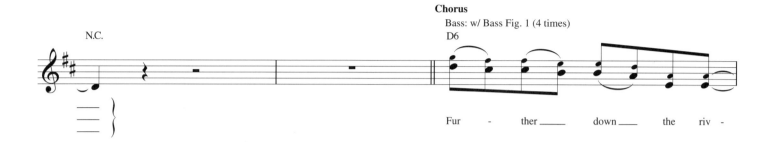

Further down the riv-

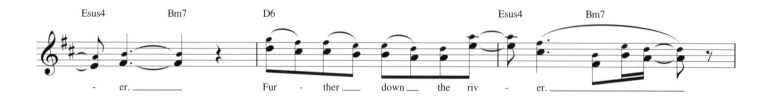

-er. Further down the riv-er.

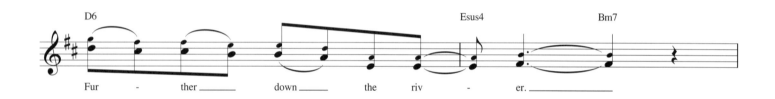

Further down the riv-er.

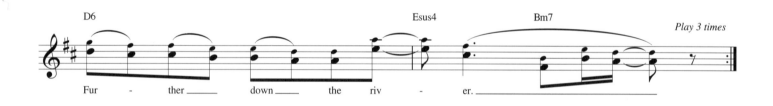

Further down the riv-er.

Outro
Bass: w/ Bass Fig. 1 (28 times)

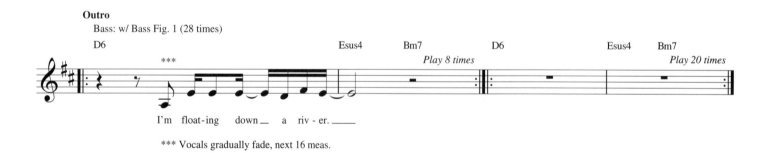

I'm floating down a riv-er.

*** Vocals gradually fade, next 16 meas.

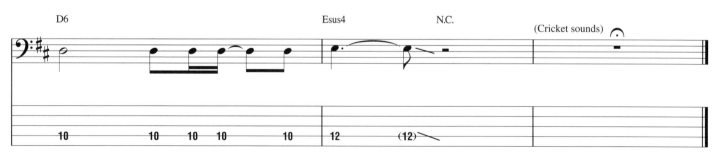